Magical History Tour

TRENCH WARFARE
AN INFERNAL FURY

FABRICE ERRE
Writer

SYLVAIN SAVOIA
Artist

PAPERCUTZ

Magical History Tour

16 "Trench Warfare: An Infernal Fury"

By Fabrice Erre and Sylvain Savoia

Original series editors: Frédéric Niffle and Lewis Trondheim
Color Prep: Luc Perdriset
Translation: Nanette McGuinness

Laura Chacón — *Mad Cave Studios Founder*
Mark London — *CEO and Chief Creative Officer*
Mark Irwin — *Senior Vice President*
Chris Fernandez — *Publisher*
Diana Bermúdez — *Cover Design*
Mark McNabb — *Production*
Wilson Ramos Jr. — *Lettering*
Stephanie Brooks — *Editor*
Mike Marts — *Editor-in-Chief*

Papercutz was founded by Terry Nantier and Jim Salicrup.

ISBN 978-1-5458-0943-3

www.papercutz.com

Printed in China
September 2024

First Printing

YAAAH!
HA HA HA!
TAKE THAT!
HEH HEH. IT WAS SMART OF US TO GET INTO THIS DITCH, ANNIE...THEY CAN'T REACH US!
HMM...THAT'S TRUE, BUT WE'RE A BIT TRAPPED HERE, TOO...LIKE IN TRENCH WARFARE.
TRENCH WARFARE?
YES, DURING WORLD WAR I, FROM 1914-1918, SOLDIERS BURIED THEMSELVES IN TRENCHES AND THE FIGHTING WENT ON FOREVER...

*ALSACE-LORRAINE WAS TAKEN BY GERMANY IN 1871, AT THE END OF THE FRANCO-PRUSSIAN WAR

HUH? WHY WERE THERE SO MANY DEATHS?
WELL, ACTUALLY...
...BECAUSE THE COMBATANTS DUG TRENCHES, THE WAR DIDN'T EVOLVE.
EACH ARMY FOUND ITSELF BLOCKED IN ITS POSITION, TRYING TO KILL THE MOST OPPOSING ENEMY SOLDIERS POSSIBLE.
AND EACH KEPT BRINGING MORE MEN AND WEAPONS, JUST TO HOLD THEIR GROUND...
...IN FRANCE, ALMOST ALL MEN AGES 18-48 WENT.
DID THEY KNOW IT WOULD BE SO AWFUL?
NO, EVERYONE THOUGHT IT WOULD BE A SHORT WAR.

IN THE BEGINNING, THE ARMIES MOVED AROUND. THE GERMANS WENT INTO FRANCE...
...BUT THE FRENCH FOUGHT A COUNTEROFFENSIVE AND PUSHED THEM BACK IN THE BATTLE OF THE MARNE.
THEN, TO AVOID LOSING THE TERRITORY THEY'D WON, THE GERMANS TOOK SHELTER, FIRST IN HOLES AND THEN BY DIGGING DITCHES THEY CALLED "TRENCHES."
AND THE FRENCH DID THE SAME TO AVOID BEING PUSHED BACK AGAIN.
THEY COULDN'T GO AROUND?
SURE. SO THEN BOTH SIDES LENGTHENED THEIR TRENCHES, FORMING LINES THAT WERE HUNDREDS OF MILES LONG!

TWO FACTIONS OPPOSED EACH OTHER. THE "CENTRAL POWERS" AND THE "TRIPLE ENTENTE."
TRIPLE ENTENTE
CENTRAL POWERS
TRENCHES
UNITED KINGDOM
GERMAN EMPIRE
RUSSIAN EMPIRE
FRANCE
AUSTRO-HUNGARIAN EMPIRE
PORTUGAL
ITALY
ROMANIA
BULGARIA
SERBIA
GREECE
OTTOMAN EMPIRE
THEY DUG TRENCHES ALONG SEVERAL FRONTS IN THE WEST AND THE SOUTH.
THE ONE IN FRANCE STRETCHED OVER 435 MILES!
WOOOW. THAT WAS A LOT OF DIRT TO CLEAR!
SO NO ONE COULD MOVE FORWARD?
NO. TO DO THAT, THEY HAD TO "BREAK THROUGH" THE FRONT. IN OTHER WORDS, CAPTURE THE ENEMY'S TRENCH.
BUT IF THEY CAME OUT OF THE TRENCH, THEY'D BE ATTACKED!
YUP. THAT'S WHY THIS WAR WAS SO LONG AND DEADLY! THEY HAD TO DEFEND THEIR POSITION AND IT WAS ALMOST IMPOSSIBLE TO CAPTURE THAT OF THEIR OPPONENT.
BANG

BUT THE ENEMY TRENCH DOESN'T LOOK VERY STRONG?
HEY! GET YOUR HEAD DOWN!
NOT AT THE START, NO. BUT THEY QUICKLY GREW INTO COMPLICATED DEFENSIVE SYSTEMS.

THERE WERE MANY LINES OF TRENCHES, WHICH WERE CONNECTED BY "COMMUNICATION PASSAGES."
IF THE FIRST TRENCH WAS TAKEN, SOLDIERS COULD SEEK REFUGE IN THE SECOND ONE, THEN THE THIRD ONE, AND SO ON.

WHY DID THEY ZIGZAG? IT'S A LABYRINTH!
PETIT BOIS TRENCH
IT WAS A WAY TO PROTECT YOURSELF FROM EXPLOSIONS OR GUNFIRE.
THEY COULDN'T COLLAPSE?
OF COURSE THEY COULD! THEY HAD TO QUICKLY BE REINFORCED WITH BAGS OF SAND, WOOD, AND EVEN CEMENT...
...THEN THEY HAD TO BUILD BUNKERS AND TOILETS. TRENCHES BECAME PLACES WHERE MILLIONS OF SOLDIERS LIVED AND DIED...
...JURY-RIGGED FORTIFICATIONS IN THE GROUND, IN A WAR WAGED WITH INCREASINGLY DESTRUCTIVE WEAPONS.

IT'S SO WEIRD. THE ENEMIES AREN'T VERY FAR APART. WE COULD ALMOST REACH THEM WITH SNOWBALLS.
YES, OFTEN ONLY A FEW DOZEN YARDS.
THE SOLDIERS COULD HEAR EACH OTHER. SOMETIMES THEY TAUNTED EACH OTHER OR SHOUTED INSULTS...
DIRTY JERKS!
CONVERSELY, THEY SOMETIMES FRATERNIZED. ON DECEMBER 25, 1914, DESPITE BEING ENEMIES, BRITISH AND GERMAN SOLDIERS EXCHANGED FOOD AND SHARED CHRISTMAS CAROLS.
THEY EVEN WOUND UP PLAYING A SOCCER GAME!
IF ONLY THEY COULD HAVE SETTLED THE WAR WITH A GAME OR A SNOWBALL FIGHT...

...BUT, SADLY, THE MILITARY COMMANDERS FROWNED UPON RARE TRUCES LIKE THESE.
THE "TOP BRASS" ONLY CARED ABOUT CAPTURING THE ENEMY TRENCH. THE TROOPS WERE SUPPOSED TO FOCUS ALL THEIR EFFORTS ON THAT, NO MATTER THEIR LOSSES.

WHAT IF THEY CAME OUT TOGETHER UNEXPECTEDLY? THEY COULD CROSS THE DISTANCE BY RUNNING QUICKLY, RIGHT?
THAT'S WHAT THEY CALLED A "SORTIE" OR AN ASSAULT...ALL THE SOLDIERS IN THE FRONTLINE HAD TO GET READY.

FIRST THEY HAD TO CLIMB OUT OF THEIR TRENCH...
...GET PAST THEIR OWN BARBED WIRE...
...RUN OVER TO THE ENEMY TRENCH...
...AND THEN CROSS MORE BARBED WIRE...
...THE WHOLE TIME, THE ENEMY WAS SHOOTING AT THEM WITH RIFLES AND, WORSE, WITH MACHINE GUNS THAT COULD FIRE 500 BULLETS PER MINUTE.
GUNFIRE MOWED DOWN ATTACKERS. SOME OF THE WOUNDED WERE ABANDONED BECAUSE IT WAS TOO DANGEROUS TO PICK THEM UP. THEY DIED ALONE ON THE BATTLEFIELD.

THAT'S AWFUL!
THAT'S WAR, NICO—TRYING TO HURT THE OTHER SIDE AS MUCH AS POSSIBLE...
...THE AREA BETWEEN THE TRENCHES BECAME A WASTELAND CALLED "NO MAN'S LAND." IT WAS IMPOSSIBLE TO CROSS.
NOTHING LIVED THERE, NEITHER MEN, NOR ANIMALS OR TREES...ONLY BARBED WIRE, SHELL CRATERS, MUD AND BODIES.

I'VE GOT AN IDEA! WHAT IF WE DIG A TUNNEL?
YES, SOME PEOPLE THOUGHT OF DOING THAT TO DEPOSIT EXPLOSIVES UNDER THE ENEMY'S TRENCH.
BUT WHEN ONE SIDE DETECTED AN ENEMY TUNNEL, THEY BUILT A "COUNTERMINE" TO DESTROY IT.
PSHHH
SOME OF THE EXPLOSIONS CREATED HOLES OVER 80 FEET DEEP!
THERE WERE ALSO COMMANDOS, "FRENCH SPECIAL FORCES," WHO SLIPPED INTO THE ENEMY'S TRENCHES FOR A SURPRISE ATTACK. BUT THAT DIDN'T CHANGE THINGS.
SO IF NO ONE COULD WIN, THEY NEEDED TO STOP!
UNFORTUNATELY, THAT'S THE OPPOSITE OF WHAT HAPPENED...

...SINCE ATTACKING DIDN'T WORK, THE IDEA WAS TO ELIMINATE THE ENEMY IN THEIR TRENCHES BEFORE THEY COULD LAUNCH AN ATTACK.
MACHINE GUNS AND RIFLES COULDN'T REACH THEM...
...BUT GRENADES, SHELLS, AND POISON GAS COULD!
GAS?!
YES, LIKE "MUSTARD GAS," WHICH BURNED THE SKIN AND LUNGS. SOLDIERS HAD TO WEAR MASKS TO PROTECT THEMSELVES.
WHAT IF THE WIND CHANGES? IT COULD COME BACK AT US!
LET'S GET OUT OF HERE!

HUGE CANNONS BOMBARDED THE ENEMY FROM AFAR.
THE GERMANS USED "BIG BERTHA," WHICH COULD REACH TARGETS ALMOST SIX MILES AWAY!
BEGINNING IN 1915, MAJOR OFFENSIVES INVOLVED FOCUSING CANNONS ON A SINGLE POINT ALONG THE FRONT TO TRY TO BREAK THROUGH AND DESTROY EVERYTHING.
FRONT
VERDUN
FRONT
THE BIGGEST CAMPAIGN TOOK PLACE IN VERDUN IN 1916.
THE GERMANS FIRED TWO MILLION SHELLS IN THE FIRST TWO DAYS...
...A BARRAGE OF FIRE!
RUN!

*FRENCH FOR "THE SACRED WAY."

I WOULDN'T HAVE BEEN ABLE TO STAND IT. I'D HAVE GONE BACK HOME!
AH, I DON'T THINK SO...
...A SOLDIER WHO REFUSED TO FIGHT WAS CONSIDERED A DESERTER. HE COULD BE SENTENCED TO DEATH!
WHAT?! SO THEN THEY RISKED THEIR LIVES EITHER WAY?!
SOMETIMES, TO FORCE SOLDIERS TO ATTACK, THEIR COMMANDERS THREATENED TO SHOOT THEM!
MOST OFTEN, THOUGH, COMMANDERS GAVE SOLDIERS ALCOHOL TO MAKE THEM LESS AWARE.
AND THEY DIDN'T DO ANYTHING?
SOME INJURED THEMSELVES, FOR EXAMPLE, BY SHOOTING THEMSELVES... BUT THEY WERE CONSIDERED DESERTERS, TOO!

*THIS IS FROM "LA CHANSON DE CRAONNE" OR "THE SONG OF CRAONNE."

ALL THAT WORE ME OUT...WHERE CAN I LIE DOWN?
WELL, HERE...
...WHAT?! ON THE GROUND? IN THE MUD AND DIRT? WITH BOMBS ALL AROUND ME?
WELL, YES...THAT'S WHAT MOST SOLDIERS DID.
BUT I'M HUNGRY AND SLEEPY! AND I WANT A HOT SHOWER!
SOME TRENCHES WERE CUT OFF FROM BEHIND. WITHOUT SUPPLIES, SOLDIERS HAD TO MAKE DO.
AND THEY COULD SELDOM WASH.
BECAUSE THEY COULDN'T SHAVE, FRENCH SOLDIERS IN WWI WERE NICKNAMED, "POILUS," OR "HAIRY MEN."
SCRATCH SCRATCH
BUT IT MEANT "BRAVE MEN," MOST OF ALL.

AND DON'T FORGET DISEASES, LICE...
RATS!
EVEN ANIMALS GOT INVOLVED!
AH, SOME ANIMALS WERE GOOD COMPANIONS— HORSES, PIGEONS...
...AND ESPECIALLY DOGS, WHO ACTED AS MESSENGERS, RAT-CATCHERS, AND FIRST-AID WORKERS...
SOME WERE EVEN DECORATED, LIKE STUBBY...
...WHO WAS MADE A SERGEANT IN THE U.S. ARMY FOR HAVING UNMASKED A GERMAN SPY IN HIS TRENCH.

TO FORGET ABOUT THEIR FEAR AND DIFFICULT LIVES, SOLDIERS DREW, SCULPTED, SANG, AND WROTE IN JOURNALS.
A CRUCIFIX MADE FROM BULLETS.
NENETTE AND RINTINTIN, GOOD LUCK DOLLS.
THE BOMB
By France
CARVED SHELL CASE
1917
TRENCH NEWSPAPER
ALUMINUM BANDS RETRIEVED FROM SHELL HEADS.

THEY COULDN'T CALL THEIR FAMILIES?
THERE WEREN'T ANY CELLPHONES THEN! THEY WROTE LETTERS, BUT THE CENSORS READ THEM...
...SOLDIERS COULDN'T SAY ANYTHING THAT MIGHT DEMORALIZE PEOPLE "IN THE REAR," CIVILIANS WHO WORKED HARD TO SUPPORT THE WAR EFFORT!
November 28, 1917
My dear Naomi,
I didn't write you yesterday because I had nothing
interesting to tell you. Today it's pretty much the same
thing. I'm in good health and everything's fine.
In your letter today, you seemed quite intrigued by the
little brass device I forgot to tell you about. It's a
machine gun belt that I altered to use for carrying my
pencils and pens in my desk. It wouldn't do for
Andre to ruin them! So then you'd say
but for I don't know.
today.
and hug everyone
Annette

SO HOW DID ALL THAT MISERY FINALLY END? WHEN EVERYONE DIED?
NO, THERE WAS A BREAK-THROUGH IN 1918.
HEY, WHERE ARE YOU GOING?
THERE WERE SOME BIG CHANGES. COME LOOK AT THE GERMAN SIDE...
...IN 1918, RUSSIA STOPPED FIGHTING AFTER A SECOND REVOLUTION. SO THE GERMANS FOCUSED THEIR FORCES ON THE WEST, ALONG THE FRENCH FRONT.
THEY WANTED TO END THE WAR, BECAUSE THEY KNEW THEIR COUNTRY WAS EXHAUSTED AND COULDN'T HOLD ON MUCH LONGER.

BUT THEY DISCOVERED THEY WERE FACING THE AMERICANS, WHO HAD COME TO HELP THE FRENCH AND THE ENGLISH.
THE U.S. ARMY WAS FRESH AND READY TO JUMP INTO BIG BATTLES.

BUT YOU TOLD ME THEY SENT ALL THEIR FORCES IN VERDUN BUT IT WASN'T ENOUGH.
THAT'S TRUE, BUT THERE WAS ANOTHER CHANGE: SUPER-MODERN TECHNOLOGICAL PROGRESS.
LOOK ON THE OTHER SIDE OF THE HILL!

TANKS AND PLANES!
BUT...THEY'RE SMALL AND FRAGILE. ARE THOSE YOUR "SUPER-MODERN" TECHNOLOGIES?
THEY WERE REVOLUTIONARY FOR THEIR TIME! AVIATION HAD JUST BEEN INVENTED AND WAS ALREADY BEING ADAPTED TO WARFARE...

...ADMITTEDLY, THE FIRST TANKS WERE HEAVY, AND IF YOU SHOT THEIR GAS TANKS, THEY CAUGHT FIRE.
BUT ONCE THE FRENCH CARMAKER RENAULT IMPROVED THEM, TANKS COULD CROSS THE "NO MAN'S LAND" AND GET PAST THE TRENCHES. THAT CHANGED EVERYTHING!

AIRPLANES WERE USED TO SPY ON ENEMY FORCES AND FOR THE FIRST AERIAL BOMBING...
...BY HAND?!
THEY INVENTED A MACHINE GUN THAT COULD SHOOT THROUGH THE PROPELLER'S ROTATION WITHOUT DESTROYING IT.
THAT'S SAFER. FOR THE PILOT, ANYWAY.
IT WAS THE START OF AERIAL COMBAT. WAR HAD SPREAD TO THE SKY, FAR FROM THE TRENCHES.
SOME AVIATORS BECOME HEROES, LIKE THE "RED BARON" IN GERMANY AND **ROLAND GARROS** IN FRANCE.

*THE CENTRAL POWERS WERE GERMANY, AUSTRIA, AND THE OTTOMAN EMPIRE.

DONG DONG DONG DONG DONG DONG
AT 11 A.M. ON NOVEMBER 11, 1918, THE BELLS RANG OUT EVERYWHERE TO ANNOUNCE THE END OF WHAT WAS ALREADY BEING CALLED, "THE GREAT WAR."
HEY, YOU CAN STOP RUNNING!
SO TRENCH WARFARE DIDN'T GO ON DURING THE WHOLE WAR?
NO, IT WAS A MAJOR PART OF WORLD WAR I, AND THE LONGEST PART, BUT IT WASN'T WHAT DETERMINED THE WAR.
TRENCH WARFARE HAS BECOME THE SYMBOL OF THE DEADLY, ABSURD BATTLES THAT TOOK THE LIVES OF SO MANY PEOPLE.

IN PARTICULAR, IT'S THE PART OF THE WAR THAT LEFT THE DEEPEST SCARS AND WE CAN'T FORGET THAT.
MANY OF THE WOUNDED SURVIVED, BUT WITH DISFIGURING INJURIES OR NERVOUS DISORDERS. SOME WERE SHAKEN FOR THE REST OF THEIR LIVES.
THE COUNTRYSIDE ALSO BORE SCARS...THE WHOLE COMBAT AREA WAS CLASSIFIED A "RED ZONE," A DEVASTATED REGION WHERE THE CADAVERS, AMMUNITION, AND POLLUTION ASSOCIATED WITH BOMBING HAD TO BE REMOVED.
PARTICULARLY IN VERDUN, THERE ARE SEVERAL LARGE CEMETERIES.
THE TREES HAVE GROWN BACK, BUT THE GROUND IS STILL LUMPY.
THESE ARE THE VESTIGES OF THE HOLES FROM SHELLS AND THE TRENCHES WHERE SOLDIERS LIVED AND DIED.

NEAR VERDUN, THE VILLAGE OF FLEURY WAS COMPLETELY DESTROYED. BUT SIGNS WERE ERECTED TO KEEP ITS MEMORY ALIVE.
TOWN HALL
SCHOOL
GROCERY
EVEN 100 YEARS LATER, BURIED OBJECTS STILL TURN UP IN MANY PLACES—SOMETIMES UNEXPLODED SHELLS. IT'S VERY DANGEROUS. YOU MUSTN'T EVER TOUCH THEM!

*OCEANIA IS A GROUP OF ISLANDS SCATTERED IN THE PACIFIC OCEAN.

WOW...I DON'T REALLY FEEL LIKE HAVING A SNOWBALL FIGHT ANYMORE.
MANY OF THE SURVIVORS BECAME PACIFISTS. THEY NEVER WANTED TO SEE WAR AGAIN...
...OTHERS, HOWEVER, THE WAR'S VIOLENCE LEFT DEEP SCARS, AND EVEN BRUTALIZED THEIR SPIRITS...
YOU KNOW, HITLER FOUGHT IN THE TRENCHES OF WORLD WAR I.
HITLER? HE WAS IN THIS WAR AND CAME OUT ALIVE?!
YES. AFTERWARDS, HE ASSEMBLED LOTS OF FORMER SOLDIERS IN HIS POLITICAL PARTY. AND EVENTUALLY HE STARTED A NEW WAR...
...WELL THEN, I GUESS I KNOW WHAT I HAVE TO DO.

WHAT'RE YOU DOING?
CHOOSING PACIFISM...
...AND A NICE CUP OF HOT CHOCOLATE INDOORS!
HEY! ARE YOU ABANDONING THIS AREA TO OUR NEIGHBORS?
WE'LL COME BACK LATER TO BUILD A SNOWMAN ONCE THEY'VE CALMED DOWN!
HA HA! GREAT IDEA.
YAAAH!

THAT'S NOT GOING TO WORK...
...YOU'RE NOT QUITE FILLING OUT THE UNIFORM...

Some People Who Made History

Guillaume Apollinaire
(1880-1918)

Guillaume was born in Rome to a Polish woman who was herself a subject of the Russian Empire. He began to live in France starting in 1887. A poet and a friend of Picasso, Derain, and Douanier Rousseau, he enlisted as a soldier in 1914, though he wasn't technically French. A week after he became a French citizen in 1916, he was wounded in the head. Weakened, he died of the Spanish flu two days before the armistice.

Otto Dix
(1891-1969)

Born in the German Empire, Otto was studying art when he enlisted in 1914. Wounded multiple times on the French and Russian fronts, he was scarred by the horrors of the trenches. As a result, he painted scenes of warfare and of soldiers with facial injuries. Under the Nazi regime, he was persecuted as a "degenerate artist," forced to fight in World War II, and then taken prisoner.

Lazare Ponticelli

(1897-2008)

Lazare was born in Italy and lied about his age to enlist in the French army in 1914. In 1915, he was forced to join the Italian army when Italy entered the war. Wounded by shrapnel, he returned to the front in 1918. Lazare died in March 2008 at the age of 110. He was dubbed the last "poilu."

The Unknown Soldier

Many soldiers vanished, their bodies torn apart by explosions or buried on the battlefield in mass graves. In 1920, to pay homage to them and allow families who couldn't bury their loved ones to do so as well, the body of an unidentified solder was buried under the Arc de Triomphe in Paris. There are similar memorials in countries like the United Kingdom, Belgium, Germany, Italy, Serbia, and Poland.

Trench Construction

Trenches and tunnels had to protect soldiers from enemy fire. Therefore, they were never dug in straight lines, so they could reduce the impact of shots and explosions.

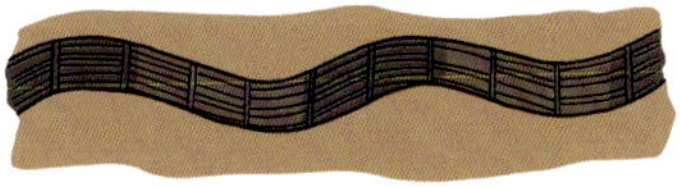

Winding trenches

Trenches had to enable a good flow of traffic. Square traverses helped soldiers pass by each other.

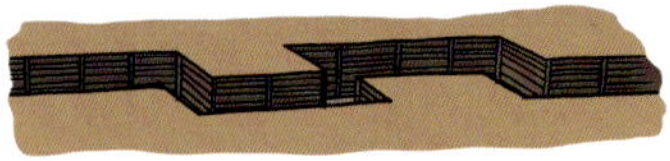

Traverse trenches

Trenches also slowed down the advance of an enemy that had reached the entrance. So the opening couldn't be visible. There could also be a fortified point at every bend or recess to block the enemy's progress.

Square traverses

Depending on the terrain, digging trenches could be very difficult. In the Alps, where the Italians and Austrians fought, trenches were dug into snow, ice, and rock at altitudes above 9800 feet!

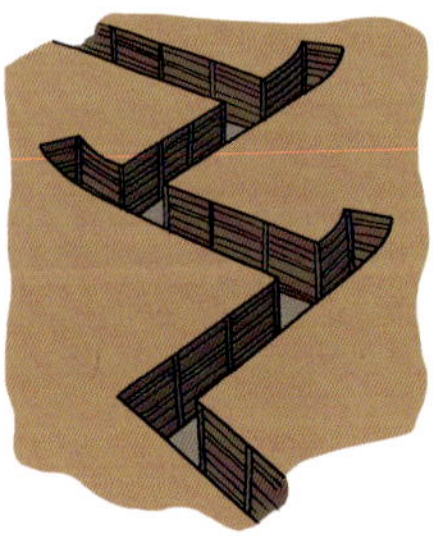

Zigzag trenches

There were trench construction manuals. The British estimated it took 6 hours and 450 men to build an 820-foot trench. At the end of the war, machines were developed to lighten the workload of the exhausted soldiers.

After the First World War, France decided to build a "super-trench" along its eastern border to protect it from further attack—a series of bunkers and armed underground tunnels named the **"Maginot Line."** But in 1940, it did not stop the German offensive, which simply bypassed it to the north.

Gear and Uniforms

Trench warfare forced armies to adjust the uniforms that soldiers wore, with helmets replacing caps for better protection against shrapnel.

The Allies

At the start of the war, French soldiers were poorly protected. Besides caps, they wore bright red pants that made them clearly visible targets for the enemy.

The French uniform at the start of the war in August 1914

The French uniform starting in Autumn 1915

At the end of 1914, they wore a "horizon blue" uniform that blended into the countryside. In 1915, they were equipped with the "Adrian" helmet, which would be adopted by almost all of France's allies:

Belgians **Russians** **Greeks** **Italians** **English**

The Central Powers

When the war began, German soldiers wore the Prussian military's spiked helmet that dated back from 1842. It was made of boiled leather ringed with iron. But the enemy could easily spot the symbolic spike, and so, starting in 1916, the old helmet was replaced with a steel one.

The Austro-Hungarian and Turkish (both allies of Germany) uniforms were very similar, apart from the Turkish helmet, the "Kabalak."

Germans **Austro-Hungarians** **Turks**

All soldiers had to have gas masks. They couldn't distinguish between the faces of their fellow soldiers and those of the enemy with the masks on.

Timeline

June 28, 1914

Archduke Franz-Ferdinand's assassination in Sarajevo leads to the threat of war.

August 1914

The great European powers declare war on each other.

July-November 1916

BATTLE OF THE SOMME

The British and French fail to break through the front. The first use of tanks.

February-October 1917

RUSSIAN REVOLUTION

The tsar is overthrown and the Communists take power.

April 1917

The US enters the war, on the side of France and England.

March 1918

Russia withdraws from the war.

SEE YOU NEXT TIME!

WHERE WILL THE MAGICAL HISTORY TOUR BRING ANNIE AND NICO NEXT?

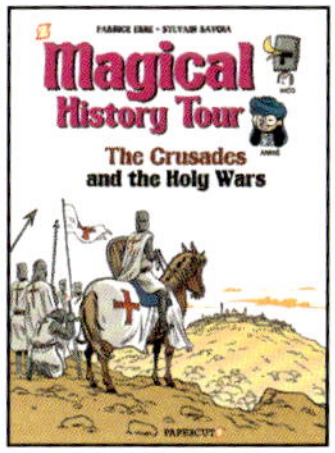

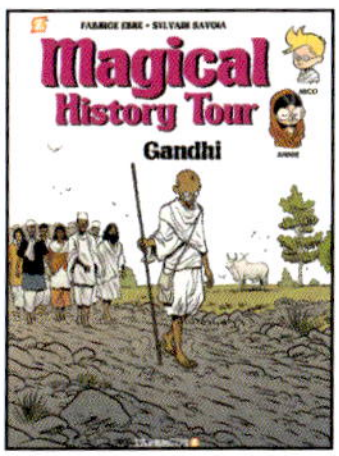

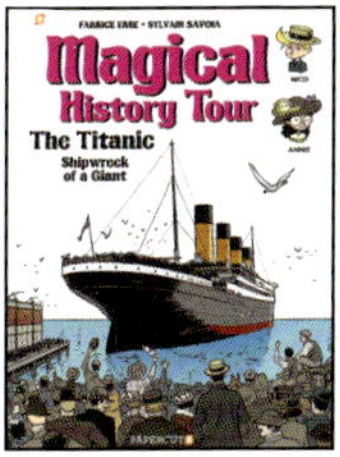

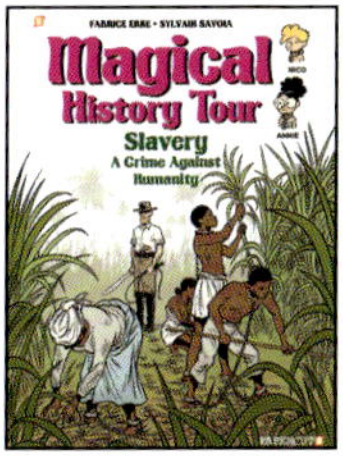

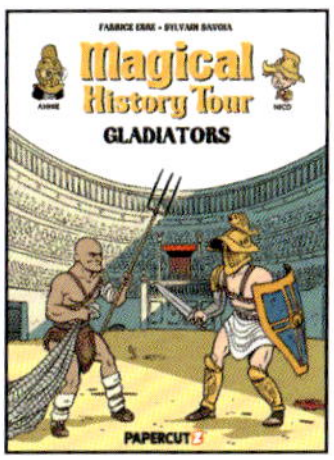

Magical History Tour

Graphic novels are available wherever books are sold and at libraries everywhere.

Fabrice Erre has a Ph.D. in History and teaches Geography and History at the *Lycée Jean Jaures* near Montpellier, France. He has written a thesis on the satirical press, writes the blog *Une anne au lycée (A Year in High School)* on the website of *Le Monde*, one of France's top national newspapers, and has published several comics.

Sylvain Savoia draws the *Marzi* series, which tells the history of Poland as seen through the eyes of a child. He has also drawn *Les Esclaves oubliés de Tromelin (The Forgotten Slaves of Tromelin)*, which won the *Academie de Marine de Paris* prize.

YAHGZ™

BY ART BALTAZAR

JOIN CRAYBI CRAYNOBI AND HIS SON, CRAYSKI CRAYNOBI, THE FUTURE CHOSEN ONE WITH THE CHOSEN NOSE, AS WELL AS THEIR MANY FRIENDS AND ALLIES LIKE WEEZERD THE WISE WIZARD, AS THEY ADVENTURE THROUGH MYTHICAL LANDS TO TRY TO SAVE THE CITY OF YAHGZ AND ITS PEOPLE, THE YAHGEEZ. BUT ARE CRAYBI AND CRAYSKI ENOUGH TO FACE THE GIANT GREEN GORILLA? OR EVEN BIGGER FOES AS THEY FORD A RIVER OF MUD, OR ENTER THE LAND OF ASHES? CRAYBI AND CRAYSKI WILL NEED THEIR WITS AND SOME HELPFUL ALLIES TO HELP EVERYONE. FIND OUT HOW THEY SAVE YAHGZ IN THIS ZANY NEW GRAPHIC NOVEL SERIES BY WORLD-FAMOUS CARTOONIST ART BALTAZAR!

PAPERCUTZ™

October 1914
The first trenches are dug in the west, on French and Belgian soil. This is the start of the "war of position."

April 1915-January 1916
BATTLE OF THE DARDANELLES
Trenches are dug in southern Europe.

April-May 1915
BATTLE OF YPRES
The first use of poison gas (mustard gas or "yperite").

February-December 1916
BATTLE OF VERDUN
The Germans don't break through the front.

July 1918
The Allies make inroads against the Germans. A return to the "war of movement."

November 1918
The armistice ends fighting.